I'M NOT EVEN THAT INTO ASTROLOGY

LINNEA BRETT

ILLUSTRATED BY CLARISSA FISCHER

Published by Ghost City Press
Syracuse, NY

Copyright © 2017 Linnea Brett
Copyright © 2017 Clarissa Fischer
Copyright © 2017 Ghost City Press

All Rights Reserved

Printed in the United States of America

First Edition September 2017

ISBN-10: 0-9964977-7-3
ISBN-13: 978-0-9964977-7-0

Cover layout and design by Clarissa Fischer
Formatted by Kevin Bertolero and Linnea Brett with text
and titles set in Avenir Next
Edited by Jo Barchi and Linnea Brett
Illustrated by Clarissa Fischer

10 9 8 7 6 5 4 3 2 1

ghostcitypress@gmail.com
www.ghostcitypress.com

table of contents

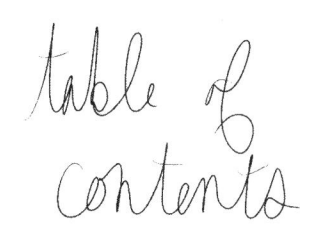

GEMINI

2   salvage
3   ii
5   it's not you, it's compulsory heterosexuality
6   iv

LEO

10   logistics
11   verbatim
12   frameworks
13   pieces of it
14   the turtle and the hailstorm
15   trajectories

LIBRA

18   bird avenue
19   not exactly a tale of triumph
21   wendt beach
22   positive mental attitude
23   the five love languages
24   dissipate

SCORPIO

28   roots
30   rust belt royalty
31   circling
33   branches
34   familiarity
37   immersion

PISCES (february)

40   rising action
41   [redacted]
42   212°
44   visibility
45   no goal
47   flux

PISCES (march)

50   the worst straight girl in the world was me at 19
51   the last two times i wanted to call you
52   the lake ontario shores parkway
54   muddling
55   black currant
57   endlessly

i'm not even that into astrology

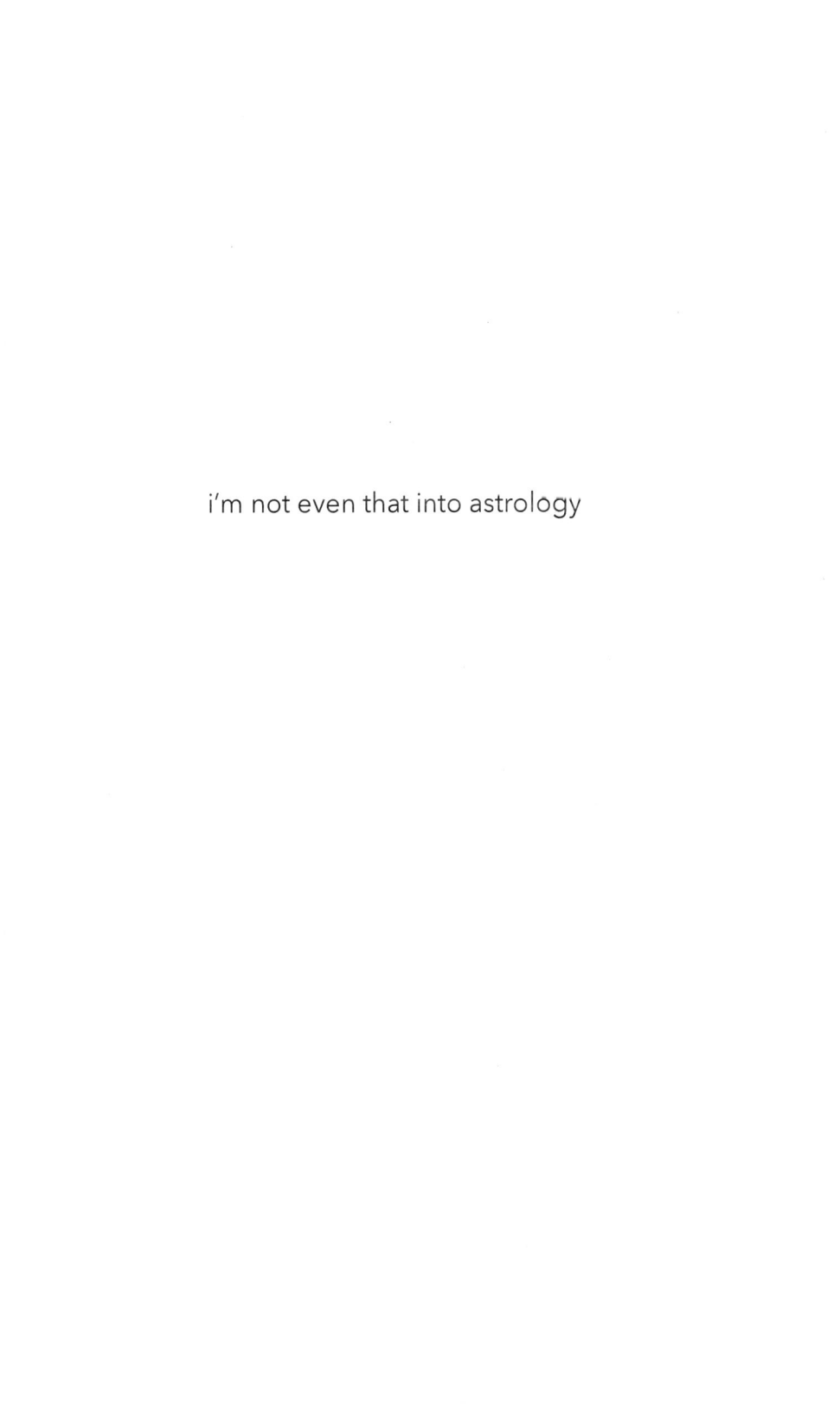

gemini

salvage

sorry i ruined our friendship
by sleeping with you
when i thought i was bisexual

in my defense
i like really thought i was bisexual

ii

i'm also sorry i framed that like it's a joke when i mean it, and that i've never apologized to you directly

both those things suck

i think we did okay staying friends
we just never talk about it and i wonder if that's hard for you

i don't ask because i know i was the villain in our story and it's easier for me to privately feel guilty than ask and risk having it confirmed or clarified

what if i was even worse than i remember

plus it's not your job to absolve me, i'm not asking for that

i'd rather just carry this around and have it loom between us and never deal with it either way and hope for the best

yeah, i know

irish catholic

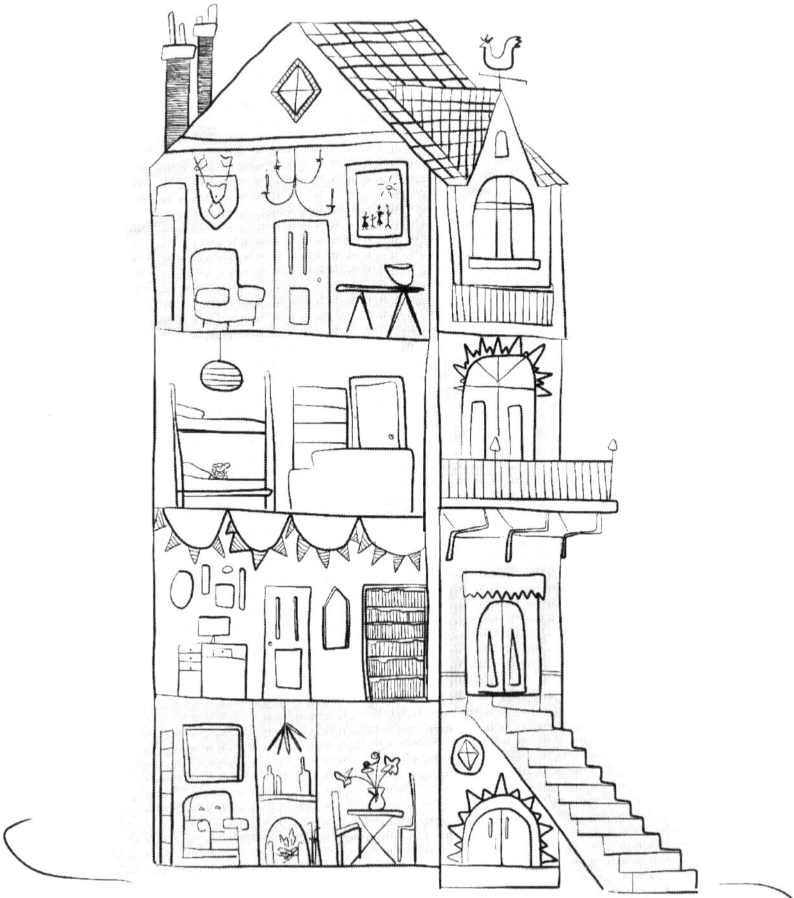

it's not you, it's compulsory heterosexuality

i spent years in ruffled dresses
spinning in circles and waiting

through all these little fairytales
under street lamps and snowflakes
the stars in july
the creek, the river
that intersection where he said
you are the only person who isn't an asshole

through boy meets girl
boy kisses girl
boy loses girl as she dissolves into panic and frustration

forced giggling and trying to soften my voice
to ignore the nausea
successfully play the character
to fall asleep before the quiet part where i have to know
this disconnect is something in me i'm too afraid to examine

queerness was the first place i could breathe and, in a world that
recognizes dykes based on a haircut i can't pull off, there is
precariousness in that relief

so your hand lingering on my lower back
feels both like a prison
and a failure

and that's how i ended up locked in the bathroom on the floor
with my head in my lap
while you sat on the couch and checked your phone

none of these things are your fault
you are just a man who has always been kind to me

iv

i don't want to make excuses
i was ungentle with you

i should have apologized the next summer but we got drunk and
you tried to kiss me
all i said was *you know i'm gay right*
that wasn't right
it made it sound like you did something wrong

the summer after that we had breakfast
i was so hungover
you across the table, suddenly
i was in the dollhouse again

it was a long time before i could sit with a man in public without
feeling like i was suffocating

fuck
you're totally going to text me about this

okay i know this is a lot
it's a lot i've never said
there's stuff you've never said, probably
and we'll get to that
but the thing is

we have to stay in each other's lives forever because we
watched all the same youtube videos in 2009 and no one else
gets our references

leo

logistics

ganson street stretches southerly from south michigan avenue
curving east to ohio street
where it ends

it's less than 4,500 feet

this matters to me enough to have measured it

the scope and direction of streets mean something to me

like your shape
and your boundaries
and your composition

and

the dimensions of the interstitial bins in the grain silos
the distance between our bedroom windows
the rail lines that connect our amtrak stations
the angles of your limbs as they change in degree
the space between you and my sheets when you arch your back

i sent you a letter once with two maps
one had the shortest route between our front doors
the other showed the quickest travel time, which was similar,
but not exactly the same
the envelope didn't follow either one, of course
the postal service doesn't work like that
they have other deliveries to make
you live in a different apartment now anyway

verbatim

> are you upset with me?
> 2:10 pm

> no not at all
> 2:11 pm

> are you upset with me?
> 2:26 pm

> no!!
> 2:29 pm

> not at all!!
> 2:29 pm

> are we fighting??????!
> 2:51 pm

> i don't know?
> 2:51 pm

> me either??????
> 2:52 pm

frameworks

i don't want to hear from you
i'm just wondering if you miss me
please send smoke signals

oh,
and if you miss me:
how much and what specifically and at which times?
how many things have you wanted to tell me?

i want to tell you everything
but i haven't figured out a way to do that without talking to you

i miss you but don't come any closer

i construct the distance between us as a task
                                as a gift
                                as an instrument
                                as a choice
                                    an end
                                    an apology

i construct the distance between us as gratitude

sometimes when i extend my arm it is to pull you closer
and sometimes it is to keep you at length
both of these are ways that i love you

pieces of it

i couldn't believe when they
i couldn't believe they noticed me
i couldn't believe

i spent so long trying to
and trying not to
and reframing
and trying

and they were so sorry
they were sorry
we were both sorry and i kept crying on my way home
and hitting the steering wheel and saying
why are you still doing this to yourself

they hurt me in places i couldn't believe
i was so grateful for the way everything sort of glowed
they hurt me in places

i couldn't believe
they hurt me

i was so grateful

they said they were sorry and i said i was sorry
and i asked them to but they shrugged and said they were sorry
and i asked them not to
but i just made myself so small and said i was sorry

there are still ways that i hurt
and there are still ways that they hurt
and i have stopped asking

but we are both still saying we are sorry

the turtle and the hailstorm

there are six funny people in the entire world
you and i are two of them

we are so lucky

we are so lucky we found each other

you said *this isn't tenable* and
i nodded then googled tenable

i google it every time
i remember that

i did just now

i know it means we don't work but
i still want the definition
it never helps

two years later you said
it sucks how you don't believe anything i say

when you don't answer my texts i assume you're with another woman
this hurts your feelings when i mention it but i'm usually right
or i'm right often enough to keep assuming it
i assume

you don't like to hear about the ways i keep myself together
not believing you is all i have sometimes

i'm in love with you in a way that completely fucks up my life
i'm so glad we're friends

tenable or not

trajectories

on the first page
i outlined the waterways between us
so if we time it right
we can stick our toes into the stream together
from 1,000 miles away

we are really good at someday

but the place we go together isn't real
and the world we built together isn't real

i think something is
or at least maybe something is

    i couldn't figure out how to keep loving you while holding all
        these pieces in my hands
    so i dropped them and we picked up where we left off
    things go pretty well when neither of us looks at the floor or
        mentions last april

        the water between us keeps freezing
    it interferes with the plans i made for feeling close to you
        without opening my heart

            or my legs

    let's not talk about any of the ways we fucked up

libra

bird avenue

a text that says
i'm thinking about your mouth and i can't sleep
and then she's at my doorstep

i don't remember which one of us sent it

we talk until we run out of language then we use our hands

the lines of her body make my jaw drop
i trace them
urgently
deliberately
in reverence

we're falling off a cliff
but pretending we haven't jumped yet
like we're still trying to decide

we think what happens next could still be up to us

not exactly a tale of triumph

i'm a shitty husband

i know that's a weird thing for a single woman to say
but hear me out

my girl wants me to take her dancing
and here's the thing:
i can't dance

and here's the other thing:
her body
it moves like there's magic involved
like she's casting a spell
or praying
or guiding the planets through the solar system

and my body
it moves like an apology
like it's a curse
or it's trying to recover from something

so on thursdays she goes
and i drink beer and yell at the tv
or whatever it is men do when they're insecure
and afraid of new experiences

anyway i went this week
then we got in a fight
because i was reading an article on my phone instead of
participating

i definitely acted like she was being unreasonable
but she kind of had a point
going is not the same as trying

20 Ω

wendt beach

we met and i think the stars were aligned
something stupid like that

we got all the fireworks and the rose petals
and the best views of the lake
but who gets to keep that forever?

we got this fruit
and we ate all the way to the rind
roveling in the juicy pulp
taking hungry mouthfuls
grinning at our own dumb luck

but then there were wilted, soggy husks
and everything was covered in snow
and everyone lost their jobs
and the sunset is so much less beautiful when it's just making
everything colder

there are only so many worlds two people can occupy together
                            before all the dishes break
            and no one wants to get out of bed to get the broom

i was sick of sweeping
    sick of being swept up
    sick of being left in a pile of dust and glass bits

for her to step in later
and wince

i have no problem admitting when i'm wrong
it will just be two years later, in a book you won't read

positive mental attitude

she needed me and i loved her and
she needed me and i loved her

we woke up and went to sleep with my love and her needs
and her needs
and my love and her needs

we met at the table and i set down dishes
she held utensils in both hands

she needed me and
i needed a minute

she needed me and
i needed to open a window

she needed me and
i needed some air

she needed me and
i needed to find my keys

she needed me and
i needed her to step out of the way and stop blocking the door

the five love languages

we're in the corner booth at amy's place and i'm outlining some details on interest rates
i haven't drawn anything on a napkin yet, but we both know that's coming
you're pretending to listen, but i know you too well to believe your nodded affirmations

you are an expert at making people feel heard without listening to them
at only keeping parts that interest you

this makes strangers feel special but the way you love me makes me so lonely
i am constantly pleading with you
trying to make you see the rest of the parts

i get the check and then we're outside and your face is up against mine and we're moments from where this always ends:

my legs and your waist
and you saying
i miss you
and me saying
i'm right here

and you saying
no, i miss you
and me avoiding eye contact and mumbling
i'm right here

dissipate

places that felt like magic when we were falling in love, i stand in now and it's like

this is just fucking bidwell park

how embarrassing

25 ♎

scorpio

roots

something that feels important to note is i am not fun

i'm fidgety and overbearing and hopelessly determined to follow rules and am, at most, 30 seconds from scolding the person standing closest to me at any given time

you're constantly reminding me *i like you exactly how you are* which is the most fucked up thing anyone has ever said

i got you five birthday presents
which felt normal until i clicked "purchase"
then i realized was out of control

i wrote different notes on each tag
tried to think of five different ways to sound clever and sexy

what i meant, but didn't write was:

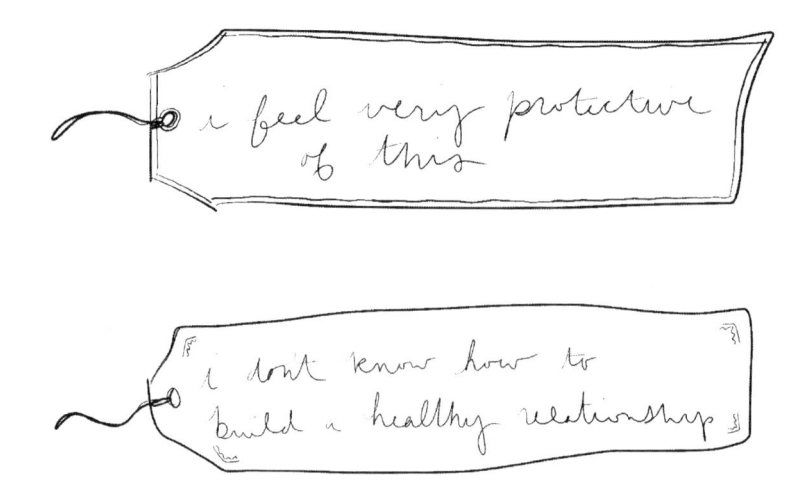

i feel very protective of this

i don't know how to build a healthy relationship

i'm not as emotionally available to you as i should be

i'm working on it

please don't give up on me

rust belt royalty

you asked if i like oysters
and i sort of absentmindedly said yes
i mean, i like seafood generally, so
i've never had them, i just didn't really think about it

but then you ordered them and they were suddenly in front of me and i had to google under the table how the fuck you eat an oyster
that stupid little fork?

look, i like you a lot and maybe it's internalized class shame but i'm not going to let you teach me how to eat an oyster on our first date

come on

i have limits

circling

one way to spend a weekend
is to lie very still
and not say anything

others involve fingertips
and eyelashes
and varying lengths of time between each breath

you do way less laundry the first way

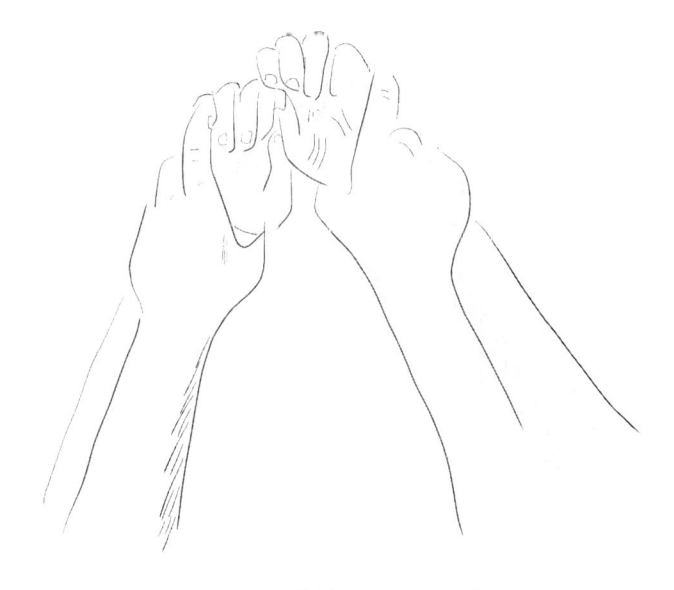

everything is so scary until i hear your voice
and then things feel totally normal which is a whole different
kind of scary

i started crying during our first kiss but i didn't mean it like that
and then i also cried when
god i'm so embarrassing

literally don't tell people that story
i know i just admitted it but i still feel self conscious

32 ♏

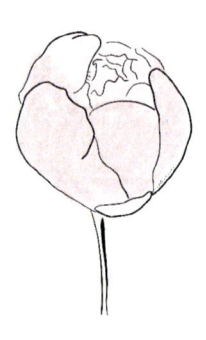

branches

every time i extend my arm and reach you i'm surprised
you've never been beyond my grasp but
maybe next time
i'm afraid of getting used to you

there are soft spots i've been hiding for so long i forgot they were part of me and i find them sometimes *i just want to feel close to you* for a minute or so *shhh sh shut up* and then they're back below the surface

you said *i want that too* and i mumbled *whatever*

it took more than a year to reach the moment i admitted *i have no idea what i would do without you*

then you said *i want clearer boundaries* and *i want to know what you want* and i rolled my eyes and said *grow up* with a smirk but i knew you were asking me for things i should be able to give you

you said *it's hard falling in love with you* and you were referring to a specific set of conditions but also, you weren't

am i reproducing the emotional violence of heteronormativity because i'm too limited to imagine different roles or patterns?

god, can we watch a movie or something?

it's suddenly really obvious that i'm a huge idiot

familiarity

you asked why i want to go to paris and i said *in 1853* and you, to your credit, didn't groan at all

the haussmannization of paris razed entire neighborhoods

they thought they could eliminate social problems through design. i want to root for environmental determinism. it's a nice idea, that you can fix everything through careful planning. i feel those yearnings

it was urban renewal before there was urban renewal, although in paris they built broad avenues and fountains and parks, and in niagara falls we got looming, alienating buildings that take up entire city blocks

when you asked about love canal i said *okay it happened in the late 70s but the story starts just before 1890* and you narrowed your eyes but you were smiling and i said *you knew i was like this when you asked the question*

so william t. love designed a utopia, which already leaves us heartsick, right - because utopia comes from two greek words meaning "no" and "place" - it's unattainable from the start

no place

he called it "model city" which is a little obvious for my taste, but this is what people did at the time, they imagined Model Cities

the idea that deliberate spaces could be enough

but back to love

it's important to me that you know that the story starts with good intentions and doesn't have a satisfying ending

there was poison and tragedy and community organizing and a national state of emergency decades of lawsuits

they renamed the neighborhood

model city exists too, technically. it's a hamlet in the town of lewiston, but the only real evidence of it is a north/south roadway called model city road. it's barely a mile long. there's a garbage disposal plant there

the best laid plans, etc. intentions don't go the way we want

planners don't seem to learn lessons, or at least not the lesson that you can't solve everything by making lists

maybe that's why i picked it; i already had the blind spot

you said *okay, so olmsted?* and *what about robert moses?* i hesitate and you say *i like hearing you talk about things that you care about*

so i tell another story about how the road paved with good intentions led us here, surrounded by highways and the leftovers of steel mills and chemical factories

obviously the world used to look different
that shouldn't take me by surprise but it does somehow nearly always

i used to be encouraged by that
i used to think more things were possible
we'll never see paris the way that it was but we're going to rehoboth in a few weeks
so i guess there are still places left

immersion

all i ever do is kiss your shoulders and then ask if i'm being annoying

no i like it

the rain starts and it ruins all our plans but we find the only open bar on the island

you tell everyone it's our wedding night and no one asks why we're alone at this bar, or why i'm wearing leggings and you're wearing a tee shirt that says "FBI: female body inspector" if we just got married

they just smile and say *young love, i remember* and *that explains all the giggling*

we get a lot of drinks for that

in the car, after, i say *my ex girlfriend would be so mad if she knew i let you do that* and your smirk takes up the rest of the ride home

we agree this will end badly, but can't decide how

we agree

pisces
(february)

rising action

do you remember that moment
on seneca street between main and pearl
when i was alive
and you were alive
and i guess there were other people there too
but it didn't really feel like it

maybe it was between pearl and franklin

then on norwood avenue
in your car

it's hard not to touch you
and it's hard not to say
it's hard not to touch you

i want to talk about what we were wearing
i want to talk about where your eyes were looking
where my eyes were looking

i want to let the summer ruin both of us
i want to burn the city down
with a series of moments
we've devoted to resisting
                    and resisting
                                and resisting

i hope we never have sex
let's just sit and stare across every table in this city at each other
and suffer

[redacted]

were we at the airport?
all i remember are your eyelids

i have lived entire lifetimes looking at your shoulders and
counting my fingertips
i've gotten pretty close, but it never really lines up right

i feel so debilitatingly unsure in your presence
that when we drove past that empty church
and you straight up said

███████████████

i spent four blocks in silence
wondering what you meant by it

we're in a fragile part and i want to keep it
so i keep not asking you any questions
and you keep not answering them

instead you do things like:
show up in my front yard and
pull me up against you
and say *i can hear you
smiling* into my ear
and then i try to
frown but i only
smile bigger

212°

we climb in together
turn the heat on
and sit here like frogs

we talk about the weekend
or our workdays
or what we want for dinner
whatever stupid thing

ignoring the hard parts
just to be around each other

neither one of us will say it

we just keep looking at it
and then looking away from it
and not calling it by its name
or mentioning the changing temperature

no, no, i get that i didn't
but neither did you

the tension is so fun some nights
then other nights are

wide eyes and exposed nerves
estimating the distance between
your feet and each of the doors

i like the version of the story where you fuck up so i move on
without bleeding or leaving all these flower petals everywhere

reality is more complicated

as i'm thinking i need to figure out a way to keep my hands off you
you look up from the bar and say *you never touch me*
and i'm reminded again how we can live through the same
thing in such different ways

43)·(

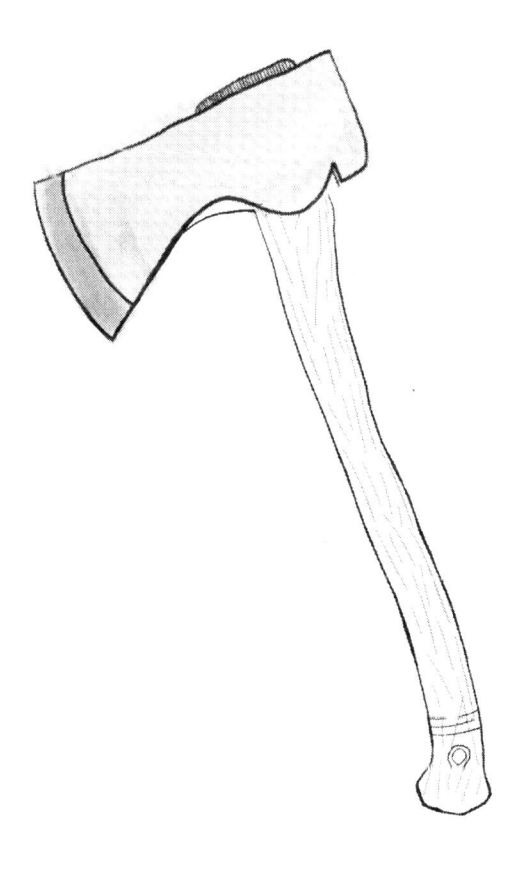

visibility

i tried to let you
i tried to show you
i tried to be vulnerable

i made you so angry
you called me
dramatic

i tried something else
i took all the writhing parts
i pulled them out

i made armor
defensive and rigid
and cold
i polish the surface

i keep the exterior smooth
controlled

it takes up so much
space
i wonder if it's my
entire self if i
contain anything soft

easy
we keep reaching impasses

your frustration meets
my panic

i spiral inward
you push forward

all rage

i bury myself farther away

you called me frigid

i try to hold on to you

i lose my grip on
myself

no goal

we talked a lot about my birthday ahead of time but then we just went to the closest restaurant

you were too hungry

i like you too much

i don't like their food

a week later i said *it isn't fair you get to check in and out based on your mood and your schedule* and you seemed surprised, even startled

you said *i'll do anything to keep you in my life, just tell me* and i think we both felt hopeful but that was months ago

i send four other women a picture i would rather send you then ask how your day is going

i miss you
or i miss when you
or i miss the idea of

i miss the way it felt before, when you were walking across the room and i was wondering if you were coming towards me

i don't know much about sports but i have a twitter account so i know sometimes a team will get like 50 points in the first half then lose the championship

i had a crush on you for like two years before you ever talked to me

i don't know, nevermind
metaphors aren't really my thing

no matter where we went or what we did
i felt so lucky to be with you

46):(

flux

there was that solar eclipse, do you remember?
maybe it was an asteroid
maybe i'm remembering wrong

you felt like that to me
inevitable
all bright lights and terror
and possibility

there were big, thick snowflakes when i typed out
i'm on elmwood, at allen, and i am not thinking about you
ok ok ok so i guess i'm thinking about you
i didn't hit send

we had a bad winter
fall was pretty rough too
summer had its own set of challenges

you hurt me more than i want to admit
to you or myself

but there was my wrist on the bar
our elbows in the convenience store
we had a couple good nights

i'm finding ways to see you that do not involve the sunrise

i am trying to be both tender and strong
i'm halfway there

it keeps resetting
i think i'm almost there
it keeps resetting
i swear i had it once
it keeps resetting
it keeps
resetting
it keeps

pisces
(march)

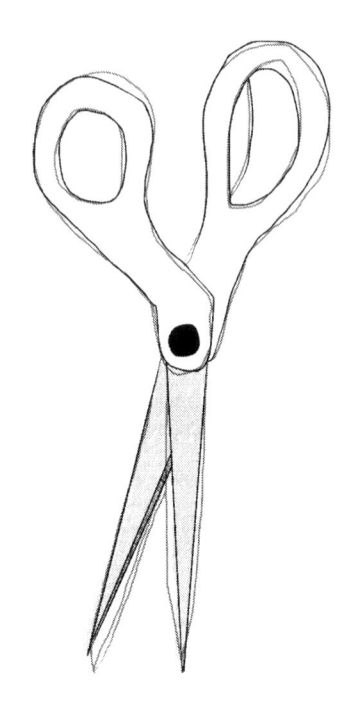

the worst straight girl in the world was me at 19

sorry i asked you to explain lesbian sex to me
then made a grossed out face at your answer

i think i made it up to you
the next summer
when i was a lot more receptive to the idea

the last two times i wanted to call you

i

the wedding was ending
and the dj played billie holiday
i remembered the first time in that hotel
i got on the bed and you said *no no not yet, not yet*

you pulled me in and pressed play

billie sang the very thought of you
and for two minutes and forty eight seconds
we were the only three people in the world

ii

after two nights apart
i returned to my cat
he greeted me with obvious relief
i thought: how chiseled that jawline is getting!
my little football head is turning into a small tiger

then i remembered i always think that after periods of separation
how i present him to you and insist:
see see, look, his face! he's totally getting definition!
and you collapse into laughter and say
no, baby no. his head is still completely round

the lake ontario shores parkway

my favorite thing to tell people about you
is that when you booked plane tickets
you got me the same seat on every flight
so i could mentally catalog the logistics of boarding ahead of time
one fewer thing to worry about

what i leave out
is how eventually that careful act of love felt so limiting
like you thought you couldn't even trust me to find a fucking numbered seat without a crisis

see, because that interrupts the narrative i like to hold
where we loved each other perfectly
at the wrong time

it brings too much to the surface
let's move on

that afternoon you drove my car across the state and i couldn't stop smiling

for the first time i knew nothing was wrong with me
i didn't know how to say that, so i just said i was happy

then later: *we have what other people wait their entire lives for*
and you smiled and i'm still not sure you knew i meant that i had been waiting for you for my entire life

in some ways i still am

do you remember the tremor in your voice?

you hesitated
the entire world held its breath between the two halves of your sentence

and then

our last interaction was the worst experience of my life
nobody had ever hurt me that badly before and no one has since

i went to the bar that night and got so fucked up
i texted the only other lesbian i knew and instead of having sex with her i ugly cried directly into her mouth

she was a libra

i run into her sometimes. she always suggests we get lunch

i don't ever see you

i know it sounds crazy but i swear
for two years my entire world existed on the lower rim of your eyelid
and then it was gone

i don't even have your phone number

but i'm not looking back for any doors
i can't hear us laughing anymore but

there are rooms inside me where your name echoes and i'd like to keep them
we can be both strangers and not strangers
we don't need all these layers

muddling

there are a million ways to tell our story
one goes:

here is every version of myself i have ever been
i said urgently, pouring the contents on the bed

indeed
she replied fondly

then in the morning when she said
we've lived this day a thousand times

i thought so too
but in a way that might have meant something different

i didn't ask her to elaborate

i mean this in the most romantic way possible:
    one way we could love each other forever
    is just to ache in the same general direction
    though i'm open to other suggestions

black currant

alternating chapters of my life might go:

>times when my room smells like you
>times when it doesn't

i have a preference

it's the strangest thing
how every time you ask me how i'm doing
suddenly everything is perfect

there are pieces of me that only know you
spaces in my brain that light up at the sound of your voice
and stay glowing for awhile
in the quiet
after you

56 H

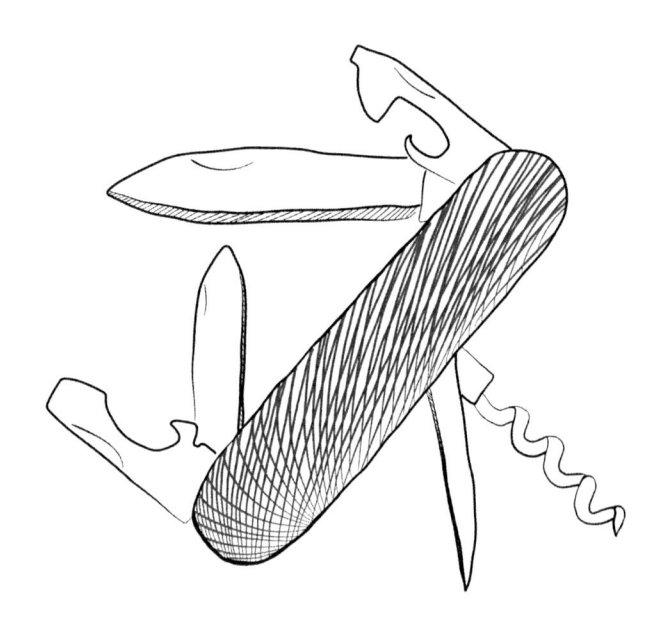

endlessly

i could write entire novels about the chances we have missed
and i still might

because i was lying next to her thinking about you
and then i was lying next to her thinking about you
and then i was lying next to her thinking about you
well, you get it

then i was next to you
and i thought *thank god i have someone else to think about,
i would be so fucked otherwise*

sure, there's aching
we both know that's part of the deal
but the aching ceases, mostly
most of the time

and the truth is

every moment i have shared space with you
has been enough

linnea brett is a lesbian who lives in buffalo, ny. she's a quintuple virgo (sun, moon, venus, mercury). this is her first book.

clarissa fischer is a queer illustrator and scorpio currently based in minneapolis, mn.

OTHER TITLES FROM GHOST CITY PRESS

Everything Dies and I Guess That's Okay, Kyla Bills
From the Estuary to the Offing, Kevin Bertolero
Tailgating at the Gates of Hell, Justin Karcher
This is a Room Where You Wait for New Language, Luis Neer
Otherwise Jesus, Blake Wallin
an uncapitalized me, Kimya Lamb
A Darker Hue of Human Truth, Richard Reyes
All Dogs are Puppies, Kyla Bills
Condominium Morte, Vince Trimboli
Saranac Lake Ghost Poems, Maurice Kenny
The Muddy Banks, Michael Begnal
Modern Thought, Kevin Bertolero
Fifth Season Fever, Davis Tate
Homebodies, Zooey Ghostly
Abuse Cycle, Ace Boggess
Lavish Applause, Marcie Hintermeister
Queen Christina, Amanda Earl
Klaatu Verata Nikto, Cooper Wilhelm
To You, Catch Business
Fables with Fangs, Christopher Morgan
Slipknot Hasn't Tweeted Since 2012, Joseph Parker Okay
Inventory, Joyce Chong
H.A.G.S., Luis Neer
Hemodynamics, Emily Sipiora
I Wish You Never Emailed Me, Alexandra Naughton
Hipster Idiot, Mallory Smart
Cry Lightning, Jordan Hoxsie
It's Fine, Joseph Barchi
Schizophrenic Genesis in the Deep Blue Jeans, Kevin Spenst
Haiku to the Chief, Gerry Crinnin
I Knew You Once, Alexandra Kesick
Bonus Zones, August Smith
It's Fine, I'm Fine, I Think I'm Fine, Amanda Dissinger
Meaning, the Shepherd of Impulse, Carter Jones
Bad Ritual, Katie Rice & Lisa Keller
Ladybug Girl & Other Poems, Roseanna Boswell

We All Have to Keep Our Heads, Sara Adams
Something Vague, Shy Watson
Not a Casual Solitude, Stacey Teague
Blythe Arizona (Motherfucker), Elijah Pearson
Until the Foxes, C.M. Keehl
American Exceptionalism for Daughters, Sara Cantwell
Puppycat, Precious Okoyomon
Friends That Can't Even, Mike Van Kennen
Highlights, C.A. Mullins
Jetty (It's A Pile of Rocks), Dalton Kamish
Faster, Theodore Fox
The Blind Kink of Lady Justice, Richard Reyes
Mother, I'd Like, Ruby Brunton
Girl Parts, Makenzi Miller
[You Look Tired], Erin Taylor
From Here 'Til Utopia, Jeremiah Walton
Old Ghost New Bones, Johnny Kiosk
The Lucidity of Giving Up, Blake Wallin
Beauty is the Mystery of Life, Manuel Arturo Abreu
other milkweed diners, Vince Trimboli
At A Crossroads With Solipsism, Georgia Beatty
We Meet By Accident, Ethan Shantie
If You Stare Long Enough, Wood Grains Will Warp, Brendan Wallace
Rotten Kid, Benjamin Brindise
American Blasphemies, Megan Kemple
Dear Dementia, M. Wright
Soft Boy, Kevin Bertolero
yr yr, Matt Margo
Origami Creature, Nathanael William Stolte
A Dream You Have Not Had, Isabelle Davis
Dream-like Houses, Joyce Chong
Thirteen, Dalton Day
Urban Nectar, Shirley Jones Luke
goddish, Kari Sonde
Daydreams in 6/6/6, Rosie Accola
Airplane Poems, Abigail King
Notes from Shower, Jake Cheriff & Camille Petricola
STOP GODDAMN APOLOGIZING, Sarah Jean Alexander
Self-Help, Nancy Tang

Welcome to Bermuda, Evan Zimmer
Shard Atlas, Wren Awry
MUSTANG, Jordan Hoxsie
Baby on Bar, Emily O'Neill
Fleeting With No Good Reason, Rivka Yeker
I Wait by the Door of Blue 52 to Come Home, Beyza Ozer
Sounds in Verbatim, Shannon Cawley
Once Upon a Time I was Micael Thomas Taren, Evan Kleekamp
Oscar Mike Alfa Romeo, J. Sebastian Alberdi
Internet Boyfriend, Christopher J. Lee
Blinding Narcissus, Robbie Coburn
How to Talk to Writers at Parties, Deirdre Coyle
Places, Christian Patterson
Conversations, Jakob Maier
Stevie Nicks Wild Heart, Dylan Lewis
Liner Notes, Katie Prout
Killer, Ashley Mares
i love you 2016, Shy Watson
Necronomincon, Sam Feldman
You Should Be Here, Amanda Dissinger
Like Love, Annette Schlichter
SCREAMS and Lavender, Dior J. Stephens
Just Because You've Been Hospitalized for Depression Doesn't Mean You're Kanye West, Justin Karcher
The Rotting Kind, Jesse Rice-Evans
Oral, Kyla Bils
To Breathe Deep, Christopher Morgan
I Don't Know What I'm Doing but I'm Doing It Loudly, Kimya Lamb
Land of Water Eaters, Luis Neer
Bathtub, Theodore Fox
Masachrist, Robert Fowler
Skillful Interiors, Rachel Davies
AVOKA, Elle Nash
!!!be less afraid!!!, El Pearson
In Search of Blue Peonies, Janea Kelly
The Ocean is Bigger than Anyone Who Has Ever Hurt You, Katie Burke
Have Trust in Being, Lander Eicholzer
//GERMZ, Stephon Lawrence
Bangers, Erin Taylor

Wild Horse Rappers, Precious Okoyomon & Willis Plummer
GRAPHIC, Rachelle Toarmino
SEACHANGE, Katie Rice & Lisa Keller
Snake Eyes, Shane O'Donnell
Flowers are for Pussies & Other White Lies, Sung Him
Rib Missing, Emily Muerhoff
Last Week's Weather Forecast Made Me Nervous, NM Esc
Acknowledgments, Clare Vernon
The Girl in the Fishbowl, Vanessa Castro
Going to Ithaca, Chrissy Montelli
Zorko, Greg Zorko
SkySea, Saquina Karla C. Guiam
How To Be A Perfect Bride, Lucy K. Shaw
When Cars Touch, Alexis Bates
To a T, Jean Yoon
Object of Art, Aiden Arata
The Coast, a Pit and a Child, Sylvia Gutierrez
Grief Nausea, Alexandra Wuest
Juice, Alyson Lewis
Green Looping Fantasy, Caroline White
Faggy Bird Poems, Joe Rupprecht
For the Love of All That's Holy, Don't Buy a Boat When Venus is in Retrograde, Brenna Mar
Torch Song, Adrian Sobol
Man as a Cactus, Jordan Alan Brown
Rub This Daisy Into My Palm, Justin Chase Jones

Please visit **www.ghostcitypress.com**
to purchase or download any Ghost City Press title.

Ghost City